RICK STEIN

Fish

Photography by SIMON WHEELER

THE MASTER CHEFS

TED SMART

RICK STEIN and his wife Jill opened The Seafood Restaurant at Padstow, Cornwall, in 1975, as a small, harbourside bistro selling locally caught fresh fish. In the past 20 years it has become one of the best-known restaurants in the UK, with an international reputation; it has won awards from all the major food guides, and was named Restaurant of the Year by *Decanter* magazine in 1989 and by Egon Ronay in 1995.

Rick Stein's first cookery book, *English Seafood Cookery*, was the Glenfiddich Food Book of the Year in 1989. He writes occasional pieces for national newspapers, among them the *Sunday Times*, the *Independent on Sunday* and the *Independent*.

Rick Stein's BBC-TV series *Taste of the Sea* was one of 1995's most successful television cookery programmes. Nominated for a number of awards, it won the Glenfiddich Television Programme of the Year Award. It was accompanied by a book of the same name, which was chosen as the André Simon Food Book of 1995.

CONTENTS

SALMON TARTARE   8

MUSSELS WITH CORIANDER,
chilli, garlic and ginger   10

GRILLED FISH SAUSAGES
with Chambéry and sorrel sauce   12

LINGUINE WITH PRAWNS,
dill and courgettes   14

SMOKED HADDOCK PASTIES
with leeks and clotted cream   16

BAKED HAKE
with a hot fennel and butter sauce   18

POACHED MACKEREL FILLETS
with mint, sherry vinegar and butter sauce   20

CHARGRILLED SEA BASS
with roasted red pepper, tomato and basil salsa 22

FILLETS OF LEMON SOLE
with salsa verde mayonnaise 24

CACCIUCCO 26

THE BASICS 28

A NOTE ON CHOOSING FRESH FISH

CLEANING MUSSELS AND CLAMS

PREPARING SQUID

FISH STOCK

MAYONNAISE

CHAMBÉRY AND SORREL SAUCE

Reach not after morality and righteousness, my friends; watch vigilantly your stomach, and diet it with care and judgement. Then virtue and contentment will come and reign within your heart, unsought by any effort of your own; and you will be a good citizen, a loving husband, and a tender father – a noble, pious man.

Before our supper, Harris and George and I were quarrelsome and snappy and ill-tempered; after our supper, we sat and beamed on one another, and we beamed upon the dog, too.

JEROME K JEROME, *THREE MEN IN A BOAT*

INTRODUCTION

I am always looking for subtle combinations of flavours; if this can be achieved with the least possible ingredients then so much the better. I am also a believer in respecting the texture of the fresh fish. With these tenets in mind, I have collected ten of my favourite recipes, some first courses, some main courses, and several to serve either purpose.

The recipes cover a variety of cooking methods, including poaching, which is an excellent way to cook oily fish like mackerel, herring, trout and sardines. Quite a lot of oil is released into the water, leaving firm, well-flavoured fish.

Another favourite is cacciucco, a marvellous Italian fish stew, although I feel rather self-conscious about producing my own version of a dish which brings with it the same sort of arguments about the correct recipe as does bouillabaisse. Some recipes include the ink from squid and cuttlefish, some don't. I think it's a good idea to use a certain amount: with the tomato it gives the stew a beautiful reddish-brown colour. Use a mixture of three or four types of white fish; avoid oily fish.

I hope these are the sort of fish dishes you are going to love and will want to cook often.

Rick Stein

SALMON TARTARE

400 G/14 OZ FRESH SALMON
    FILLET, SKINNED
125 G/4 OZ SMOKED SALMON
1 LARGE GARLIC CLOVE, VERY
    FINELY CHOPPED
3 SHALLOTS, VERY FINELY CHOPPED
1 TABLESPOON FRESH LEMON JUICE
½ TEASPOON SALT
12 TURNS OF THE BLACK PEPPER
    MILL
PINCH OF CAYENNE PEPPER
FEW DROPS OF WORCESTERSHIRE
    SAUCE

TO GARNISH
24–32 SPRIGS OF LAMBS' LETTUCE
EXTRA VIRGIN OLIVE OIL
BALSAMIC VINEGAR
COARSE SEA SALT
COARSELY GROUND BLACK PEPPER

SERVES 4

Cut the salmon fillet and smoked salmon into very small dice. Place in a bowl, add the remaining ingredients and mix well.

Line four 8 cm/3 inch ramekins or similar containers with clingfilm, leaving the edges overhanging. Divide the salmon mixture between the ramekins and press down lightly, so that the tops are smooth. Now invert the ramekins into the centre of four large dinner plates – the bigger the better. Remove the ramekins and the clingfilm.

Arrange 6–8 sprigs of lambs' lettuce around the edge of each plate. Drizzle the rest of the plate, and the leaves, with a little olive oil, add a few drops of balsamic vinegar in between the streaks of oil, and then sprinkle with a little sea salt and black pepper. Serve at once, with a bowl of extra salad if you wish.

MUSSELS WITH CORIANDER,
chilli, garlic and ginger

2.3 LITRES/4 PINTS MUSSELS
1 TABLESPOON THAI FISH SAUCE
JUICE OF 1 LIME
1 GARLIC CLOVE, FINELY CHOPPED
1 FRESH RED CHILLI, SEEDED AND
  FINELY CHOPPED
2 TEASPOONS FINELY CHOPPED
  FRESH GINGER
2 TABLESPOONS SESAME OIL
1 BUNCH OF SPRING ONIONS,
  THINLY SLICED
2 TABLESPOONS ROUGHLY CHOPPED
  FRESH CORIANDER

SERVES 4

Clean the mussels (page 28) and
place in a large saucepan with the
fish sauce, lime juice, garlic, chilli,
ginger and sesame oil. Cover and
cook over a high heat for
3 minutes or until the mussels
have opened.

Scatter over the sliced spring
onions and chopped coriander and
turn everything over in the pan.
Serve at once.

GRILLED FISH SAUSAGES
with Chambéry and sorrel sauce

325 G/12 OZ WHITE FISH FILLETS
  (LEMON SOLE, WHITING,
  POLLACK), SKINNED AND BONED
50 G/2 OZ FRESH CRAB MEAT
4 SCALLOPS, WITH THE CORALS
1 EGG WHITE
SALT AND FRESHLY GROUND BLACK
  PEPPER
150 ML/¼ PINT DOUBLE CREAM,
  CHILLED
PINCH OF CAYENNE PEPPER
1 TABLESPOON ROUGHLY CHOPPED
  FRESH CHERVIL
A LITTLE SUNFLOWER OIL

TO SERVE
CHAMBÉRY AND SORREL SAUCE
  (PAGE 30)

SERVES 4
Cut the white fish into small pieces and place in a food processor. Chill in the refrigerator for 30 minutes. Cut the crab meat, scallops and corals into about 1 cm/½ inch pieces and chill.

After 30 minutes, add the egg white and seasoning to the white fish and process until smooth. With the machine running, pour in the cream in a steady stream, making sure that you complete this stage within 10 seconds (if over-processed, the mixture tends to curdle). Season the crab and scallops with salt, pepper and cayenne, then fold into the fish mixture together with the chervil.

Divide the mixture into eight and spoon on to eight pieces of clingfilm, placing the mixture slightly to one side. Form the mixture into sausage shapes, about 12 cm/5 inches long, then carefully roll up in the clingfilm, twisting the ends firmly to seal.

Fill a large, deep frying pan with water and bring to a gentle simmer. Reduce the heat and poach the sausages for 8 minutes. Transfer the sausages to a bowl of cold water and leave for 2 minutes. Lift the sausages out of the water, remove the clingfilm and brush each sausage with a little oil.

Preheat the grill to medium. Grill the sausages for 8 minutes, turning occasionally, until golden. Serve on warmed plates, with a little of the Chambéry and sorrel sauce spooned around them.

LINGUINE WITH PRAWNS,
dill and courgettes

2 COURGETTES

SALT AND FRESHLY GROUND BLACK
PEPPER

225 G/8 OZ DRIED LINGUINE PASTA

2 TABLESPOONS EXTRA VIRGIN
OLIVE OIL

175 G/6 OZ COOKED PEELED
PRAWNS, THAWED IF FROZEN

1 TABLESPOON CHOPPED FRESH
DILL

SERVES 4

Trim the ends of the courgettes, then cut across the courgettes to make 4 cm/1½ inch pieces; cut each piece lengthways into 3 mm/⅛ inch thick slices, then cut each slice lengthways into 3 mm/⅛ inch batons.

Place 1.7 litres/3 pints water in a large saucepan, add 3 teaspoons salt and bring to the boil. Add the pasta, bring back to the boil and boil for 10 minutes or until *al dente* – just tender but still slightly firm to the bite.

When the pasta is almost ready, warm the olive oil in a small saucepan over a low heat. Add the courgettes and cook gently for 1 minute, but don't let them fry. Add the prawns and heat through for about 30 seconds, then add the dill and season to taste. Drain the pasta, tip into a large bowl and add the prawn mixture. Toss together and serve at once.

SMOKED HADDOCK PASTIES
with leeks and clotted cream

900 G/2 LB CHILLED PUFF PASTRY
A LITTLE FLOUR
325 G/12 OZ SKINNED UNDYED
   SMOKED HADDOCK
175 G/6 OZ CLEANED LEEKS
275 G/10 OZ PEELED POTATOES,
   BOILED
4 TABLESPOONS CLOTTED CREAM
1 TEASPOON SALT
10 TURNS OF THE BLACK PEPPER
   MILL
1 EGG, BEATEN

MAKES 6

Cut the pastry into six equal pieces. On a lightly floured surface, roll out each piece to about 20 cm/ 8 inches square, then cut out six 19 cm/7½ inch circles.

Preheat the oven to 200°C/ 400°F/Gas Mark 6.

Cut the smoked haddock into 2.5 cm/1 inch pieces. Slice the leeks and cut the potatoes into 1 cm/½ inch cubes. Mix together the haddock, leeks, potatoes, clotted cream, salt and pepper.

Divide the fish mixture between the circles of pastry. Moisten one half of each pastry edge with a little beaten egg, bring both edges together over the top of the filling and pinch together well to seal. Crimp the edge of each pasty decoratively between the fingers, transfer to a lightly greased baking sheet and brush all over with more beaten egg. Bake for 35 minutes. Serve hot or cold.

BAKED HAKE
with a hot fennel and butter sauce

225 G/8 OZ UNSALTED BUTTER

2 FENNEL BULBS, TRIMMED AND
SLICED INTO ARC-SHAPED PIECES

1 ONION, CHOPPED

1 GARLIC CLOVE, CHOPPED

300 ML/½ PINT FISH OR LIGHT
CHICKEN STOCK

2 TABLESPOONS DRY WHITE WINE

1 TEASPOON SALT

10 TURNS OF THE BLACK PEPPER
MILL

1 BUNCH OF FENNEL HERB

4 HAKE STEAKS, ABOUT 225 G/8 OZ
EACH

2 TABLESPOONS PERNOD OR
RICARD

2 TEASPOONS FRESH LEMON JUICE

2 EGG YOLKS

SERVES 4

Preheat the oven to 200°C/400°F/
Gas Mark 6.

Melt 25 g/1 oz of the butter in
a shallow flameproof dish. Add the
fennel, onion and garlic and fry for
about 5 minutes or until the
vegetables are soft but not
browned. Add the stock, wine, salt
and pepper and simmer gently for
15 minutes.

Set aside four sprigs of the
fennel herb for the garnish.
Remove any large stalks and
roughly chop the remainder.

Season the hake on both sides,
lay it on top of the fennel and
onion mixture and bake in the
oven for 15–20 minutes.

Lift the hake off the fennel
mixture to a warmed plate and
keep hot. Remove a quarter of the
fennel and place in a liquidizer
with the Pernod or Ricard, lemon
juice and egg yolks.

Melt the remaining butter in a
saucepan. When it begins to
bubble, turn on the liquidizer and
blend the contents for 1 minute.
Then slowly pour the hot butter
through the hole in the top of the
liquidizer goblet. Pour the sauce
into a bowl, stir in the chopped
fennel herb and season to taste.

To serve, spoon the remaining
baked fennel mixture on to four
warmed plates. Rest the hake
steaks partly on the fennel. Spoon
some of the butter sauce over the
hake and the rest of the plate.
Garnish with the reserved fennel
sprigs and serve at once.

POACHED MACKEREL FILLETS
with mint, sherry vinegar and butter sauce

1 TABLESPOON SALT
4 MACKEREL, ABOUT 175 G/6 OZ
   EACH, FILLETED

SAUCE
225 G/8 OZ UNSALTED BUTTER
2 EGG YOLKS
1 TEASPOON LEMON JUICE
A GOOD PINCH OF CAYENNE
   PEPPER
10 TURNS OF THE BLACK PEPPER
   MILL
½ TEASPOON SALT
2 TABLESPOONS SHERRY VINEGAR
1 SHALLOT, VERY FINELY CHOPPED
1 TABLESPOON CHOPPED FRESH
   MINT

TO GARNISH
SPRIGS OF MINT

SERVES 4
For the sauce, first clarify the butter by placing it in a small saucepan and heating it gently for a few minutes until it has melted and the solids have fallen to the bottom of the pan. Carefully pour off the clear butter and reserve. Discard the solids.

Half fill a saucepan with water and bring to the boil. Reduce to a simmer and rest a bowl over the pan. Add the egg yolks and 2 tablespoons water and whisk until voluminous and fluffy.

Remove the bowl from the heat and gradually whisk in the clarified butter, building up an emulsion as if making mayonnaise. Add the lemon juice, cayenne pepper, black pepper and salt.

Place the sherry vinegar and shallot in a small saucepan, bring to the boil and boil until reduced to 1 teaspoon. Stir into the warm butter sauce with the chopped mint. Keep warm in a bowl of warm water.

Bring 600 ml/1 pint water and 1 tablespoon salt to the boil in a large frying pan. Reduce to a simmer, add the mackerel fillets and poach for 3 minutes, turning them after 1½ minutes. Lift out with a slotted fish slice and serve on warmed plates, with the sauce spooned around. Garnish with sprigs of mint.

CHARGRILLED SEA BASS
with roasted red pepper, tomato and basil salsa

4 SMALL SEA BASS, 400–450 G/
  14 OZ–1 LB EACH, CLEANED AND
  SCALED
2 TABLESPOONS OLIVE OIL
COARSE SEA SALT AND FRESHLY
  GROUND BLACK PEPPER

SALSA

1 RED PEPPER
1 TABLESPOON EXTRA VIRGIN OLIVE
  OIL
2 TOMATOES, SKINNED AND SEEDED
½ RED ONION, PEELED
2 FRESH RED CHILLIES, SEEDED AND
  FINELY CHOPPED
1 LARGE GARLIC CLOVE, VERY
  FINELY CHOPPED
2 TABLESPOONS CHOPPED FRESH
  PURPLE BASIL
1 TABLESPOON FRESH LEMON JUICE

SERVES 4

Preheat the oven to 220°C/425°F/
Gas Mark 7.

For the salsa, rub the outside of
the pepper with a little of the olive
oil and roast for 15–20 minutes or
until soft and slightly blackened.
Place in a plastic bag, seal tightly
and leave to cool. When cool, the
skin should come off easily. Cut
the pepper in half and discard the
seeds. Cut the red pepper flesh,
tomatoes and red onion into 1 cm/
½ inch pieces. Place in a bowl and
mix in the chillies, garlic, basil,
lemon juice, the remaining olive
oil, and salt and pepper to taste. Set
aside while you cook the fish.

Make three diagonal slashes in
both sides of each fish, then brush
with olive oil and season with sea
salt and black pepper. Brush a
ridged cast-iron griddle with a
little oil, place over a high heat and
leave until very hot. Add the fish
and cook for 4½–5 minutes on
each side. Alternatively, preheat a
grill to very hot and cook the fish
on an oiled grill pan. Serve hot,
with the salsa.

FILLETS OF LEMON SOLE
with salsa verde mayonnaise

1 LOAF OF SLIGHTLY STALE BLACK
   OLIVE CIABATTA BREAD
50 G/2 OZ PLAIN FLOUR
2 LARGE EGGS, BEATEN
VEGETABLE OIL FOR DEEP-FRYING
12 LEMON SOLE FILLETS, ABOUT
   65 G/2½ OZ EACH, SKINNED

SALSA VERDE MAYONNAISE

3 TABLESPOONS ROUGHLY CHOPPED
   FRESH PARSLEY
1 TABLESPOON ROUGHLY CHOPPED
   FRESH MINT
3 TABLESPOONS CAPERS
6 ANCHOVY FILLETS
1 GARLIC CLOVE, CRUSHED
1 TEASPOON DIJON MUSTARD
1 TABLESPOON FRESH LEMON JUICE
½ TEASPOON SALT
6 TABLESPOONS MAYONNAISE
   (PAGE 29)

TO SERVE

LEMON WEDGES

SERVES 4

For the salsa verde mayonnaise, put
the parsley, mint, capers, anchovies,
garlic, mustard, lemon juice and salt
into a pestle and mortar or food
processor and grind to a coarse
paste. Stir into the mayonnaise and
season with a little more salt if
required. Set aside.

Break the ciabatta bread into
small pieces. Place in a food
processor and process into crumbs
– they do not need to be too fine –
then turn out on to a large plate.
Spoon the flour on to another
plate and pour the beaten eggs into
a shallow dish.

Heat the oil for deep-frying to
190°C/375°F or until a cube of
bread browns in 30 seconds.
Preheat the oven to 150°C/300°F/
Gas Mark 3. Line a large baking
sheet with paper towels.

Season the lemon sole fillets
with a little salt and pepper. Dip
the fillets into the flour, then into
the beaten egg and then the
breadcrumbs, pressing them on
well to give an even coating.
Deep-fry, two pieces at a time, for
2 minutes or until crisp and
golden. Remove to the baking
sheet and keep hot in the oven
while you cook the rest. Serve at
once, with the salsa verde
mayonnaise and lemon wedges.

CACCIUCCO

1 LOAF OF CIABATTA BREAD
150 ML/5 FL OZ OLIVE OIL
5 GARLIC CLOVES
3.2 KG/7 LB WHITE FISH (JOHN DORY, GURNARD, COD), FILLETED
1 COOKED LOBSTER
450 G/1 LB SQUID, CLEANED (PAGE 28)
1 LARGE ONION, CHOPPED
1 LARGE CARROT, FINELY CHOPPED
2 STICKS OF CELERY, FINELY CHOPPED
300 ML/10 FL OZ RED WINE
400 G/14 OZ CANNED TOMATOES
2 BAY LEAVES
2–3 FRESH RED CHILLIES, SLIT OPEN
6 FRESH SAGE LEAVES
900 G/2 LB MUSSELS, CLEANED AND OPENED (PAGE 28)

SERVES 8–10

Preheat the oven to 200°C/400°F/ Gas Mark 6.

Cut the ciabatta into 1 cm/½ inch thick slices, place on a baking sheet and drizzle with about 2 tablespoons olive oil. Bake for 20 minutes or until crisp. Rub a halved garlic clove over the bread.

Cut the fish into 4 cm/1½ inch thick slices. Remove the meat from the lobster and reserve the shell. Slice the squid into rings.

Heat half of the remaining oil in a large saucepan. Fry the onion, carrot and celery for 7–8 minutes, until beginning to brown. Add the wine, lobster shell, tomatoes, bay leaves, chillies and 2.3 litres/4 pints water. If you have any squid ink sacs, mash one with a little water and add. Bring to the boil and simmer for 45 minutes.

Pour the liquid through a sieve into another large pan and press with a ladle to extract as much flavour and liquid as possible.

Slice the remaining garlic. Heat the remaining oil in the cleaned pan, add the sage and garlic and fry for 1 minute. Add the squid and fry for 2 minutes, then remove and keep warm. Add the stock and fish, bring to the boil and simmer for 2 minutes. Add the lobster meat, the fried squid, the mussels and their strained cooking liquid and simmer for 1 minute.

To serve, lay two slices of the crisp bread in the bottom of each plate and ladle the soup on top.

THE BASICS

A NOTE ON CHOOSING FRESH FISH

The eyes should be bright with no red flushes, the skin should be bright, the gills should be a fresh pink or red, not brown. The smell should be welcoming, not fishy. If choosing fillets they should be white, not yellowing. Use the freshest-looking fish on the slab as a yardstick to judge the others.

Ask your fishmonger to prepare the fish for you for the recipes in the book, but remember to ask for the bones to make a good, simple fish stock. It is particularly worthwhile asking the fishmonger to scale the fish, since scales tend to fly all over the kitchen. However, you will need to check that all the scales have been removed, by scraping from the tail to the head with a blunt knife, holding the fish under running cold water.

CLEANING MUSSELS AND CLAMS

Wash the mussels in plenty of cold water and discard any that are open and show no signs of closing again when tapped. Scrape off any barnacles with a knife and pull out the beards. Clams do not have beards, but the shells should be thoroughly scrubbed to remove all sand and mud.

To open, place in a large saucepan with a splash of water or wine, cover and cook over a high heat for about 3 minutes, shaking the pan occasionally until the shells have opened. Discard any that remain closed. Strain the cooking liquid through a muslin-lived sieve and reserve.

PREPARING SQUID

Gently pull the head away from the body – the intestines will come away with the head, which is joined to the tentacles. Reach into the body and pull out the rest of the insides: the plastic-like quill, possibly some soft white roe and an ink sac. Reserve the sac and discard the rest.

Detach the fins; pull off the purple skin from body and fins. Wash out the body with cold water. Slice off the tentacles; discard the rest of the head.

FISH STOCK

1 KG/2¼ LB FISH BONES – NOT
FROM OILY FISH
1 ONION, CHOPPED
1 STICK OF CELERY, CHOPPED
2 SMALL CARROTS, CHOPPED
25 G/1 OZ BUTTON MUSHROOMS,
SLICED
1 TEASPOON CHOPPED FRESH
THYME

Place the fish bones in a large saucepan with 2.3 litres/4 pints water, bring to the boil and simmer very gently for 20 minutes. Strain through a muslin-lined sieve into a clean pan, add the vegetables and thyme and bring back to the boil. Simmer for 35 minutes, until reduced to about 1.2 litres/2 pints. Strain once more. The stock is now ready to use or store.

MAYONNAISE

2 EGG YOLKS
2 TEASPOONS WHITE WINE VINEGAR
½ TEASPOON SALT
300 ML/10 FL OZ OLIVE OIL

Before you start, make sure all the ingredients are at room temperature. Put the egg yolks, vinegar and salt into a mixing bowl; place the bowl on a tea towel, to stop it slipping around. Using a wire whisk, gradually beat the oil into the egg mixture, a little at a time, until you have incorporated it all.

CHAMBÉRY AND SORREL SAUCE

300 ML/½ PINT FISH STOCK
(PAGE 29)
75 ML/3 FL OZ DOUBLE CREAM
2 TABLESPOONS CHAMBÉRY DRY
VERMOUTH
15 G/½ OZ FRESH SORREL LEAVES
40 G/1½ OZ UNSALTED BUTTER
1 TEASPOON FRESH LEMON JUICE
SALT

Place the fish stock, half the cream and the vermouth in a saucepan. Bring to the boil and boil rapidly until reduced to about 100 ml/3½ fl oz. Meanwhile, wash and remove the stalks from the sorrel, then slice the leaves very thinly.

Just before serving, add the remaining cream, butter and lemon juice to the reduced sauce and boil for about 1 minute, to reduce a little more. Stir in the shredded sorrel and serve at once.

This sauce – based on a simple cream, fish stock and wine reduction – is one I make for various fish dishes.

THE MASTER CHEFS

SOUPS
ARABELLA BOXER

MEZE, TAPAS AND ANTIPASTI
AGLAIA KREMEZI

PASTA SAUCES
GORDON RAMSAY

RISOTTO
MICHELE SCICOLONE

SALADS
CLARE CONNERY

MEDITERRANEAN
ANTONY WORRALL THOMPSON

VEGETABLES
PAUL GAYLER

LUNCHES
ALASTAIR LITTLE

COOKING FOR TWO
RICHARD OLNEY

FISH
RICK STEIN

CHICKEN
BRUNO LOUBET

SUPPERS
VALENTINA HARRIS

THE MAIN COURSE
ROGER VERGÉ

ROASTS
JANEEN SARLIN

WILD FOOD
ROWLEY LEIGH

PACIFIC
JILL DUPLEIX

CURRIES
PAT CHAPMAN

HOT AND SPICY
PAUL AND JEANNE RANKIN

THAI
JACKI PASSMORE

CHINESE
YAN-KIT SO

VEGETARIAN
KAREN LEE

DESSERTS
MICHEL ROUX

CAKES
CAROLE WALTER

COOKIES
ELINOR KLIVANS

THE MASTER CHEFS

This edition produced for The Book People Ltd,

Hall Wood Avenue, Haydock, St Helens WA11 9UL

First published in 1996 by

WEIDENFELD & NICOLSON

THE ORION PUBLISHING GROUP

ORION HOUSE

5 UPPER ST MARTIN'S LANE

·LONDON WC2H 9EA

ISBN 0 297 83651 X

DESIGNED BY THE SENATE

EDITOR MAGGIE RAMSAY

FOOD STYLIST JOY DAVIES

ASSISTANT KATY HOLDER